Jackie Robinson
Hometown Hero

Dona Herweck Rice

Consultants

Regina Holland, Ed.S., *Henry County Schools*
Christina Noblet, Ed.S., *Paulding County School District*
Jennifer Troyer, *Paulding County Schools*
Michele M. Celani, M.S.Ed., *Baldwin County Public Schools*

Publishing Credits

Rachelle Cracchiolo, M.S.Ed., *Publisher*
Conni Medina, M.A.Ed., *Managing Editor*
Emily R. Smith, M.A.Ed., *Series Developer*
Diana Kenney, M.A.Ed., NBCT, *Content Director*
Torrey Maloof, *Editor*
Courtney Patterson, *Multimedia Designer*

Image Credits: Cover and p.1 Bettmann/Corbis, LOC [LC-DIG-highsm- 21984]; p.2 Associated Press; p.5 mediaphotos/Getty Images, Associated Press; p.6 Kidwiler Collection/Getty Images; p.7 Afro Newspaper/ Gado/Getty Images; pp.2,8 LOC [LC-DIG-fsac-1a33894]; pp.3,9, 11 Hulton Archive/Getty Images; p.12 Archive Photos/Getty Images; p.10 Los Angeles Times/Getty Images; p.12 LOC [LC-USF33-012657-M3]; pp.2, 13-14 Courtesy of Brandon Jacobs; p.15 The Jackie Robinson Foundation; p.17 Associated Press, Transcendental Graphics/Getty Images; p.18 PhotoQuest/Getty Images; pp.19,20,31 Sports Studio Photos/Getty Images; p.20 Transcendental Graphics/Getty Images; p.21 Everett Collection Historical / Alamy Stock Photo; p.22 LOC [LC-USZ62-119888]; p.23 Rich Pilling/Getty Images; pp.24,32 LOC [LC-USZ62-126559]; pp.3,25 Dennis MacDonald / age fotostock/Superstock; p.27 D Dipasupil/Getty Images, Mark Sullivan/Getty Images; p.28 Photo File/ Getty Images; All other images iStock and Shutterstock.

Library of Congress Cataloging-in-Publication Data

Names: Rice, Dona.
Title: Jackie Robinson : hometown hero / Dona Herweck Rice.
Description: Drive Huntington Beach, CA : Teacher Created Materials, Inc.,
  [2017] | Includes index.
Identifiers: LCCN 2015042499 | ISBN 9781493825608 (pbk.)
Subjects: LCSH: Robinson, Jackie, 1919-1972--Juvenile literature. | Baseball
  players--United States--Biography--Juvenile literature. | African American
  baseball players--Biography--Juvenile literature.
Classification: LCC GV865.R6 R54 2017 | DDC 796.357092--dc23
LC record available at http://lccn.loc.gov/2015042499

Teacher Created Materials

5301 Oceanus Drive
Huntington Beach, CA 92649-1030
http://www.tcmpub.com

ISBN 978-1-4938-2560-8

© 2017 Teacher Created Materials, Inc.

9

Table of Contents

25

42

Let's Go, Jackie!

"Come on, Jackie! Let's go!" called Mack Robinson over his shoulder. Jackie stretched his legs to keep up. He was five years younger than his big brother. Mack ran like the wind, and Jackie wanted to run like that, too.

Happy Birthday

Jack Roosevelt Robinson was born on January 31, 1919, in Cairo, Georgia.

January						1919
SUN	MON	TUE	WED	THU	FRI	SAT
			1	2	3	4
5	6	7	8	9	10	11
12	13	14	15	16	17	18
19	20	21	22	23	24	25
26	27	28	29	30	31	

Mack's fast feet would take him far. They would take him all the way to a silver medal in the Olympics! But Jackie's legs took him even further. They took him into the hearts of people everywhere.

Mack (Matthew) wins a silver medal in the 1936 Olympics.

There are many ways to be a **hero**. How many are there? There are at least 42. Why? That was the number on Jackie Robinson's baseball uniform!

People may wonder how a ballplayer can be a hero. Playing ball well can make a good athlete. It does not make a hero. But standing strong to make things better for all players and the world does make a hero. That is what Jackie did. Some say he is one of the greatest players of all time. Many say he is one of the greatest men of all time.

Number Up!

Why are there numbers on uniforms? Numbers help referees know the players. They are easier to read on uniforms than names.

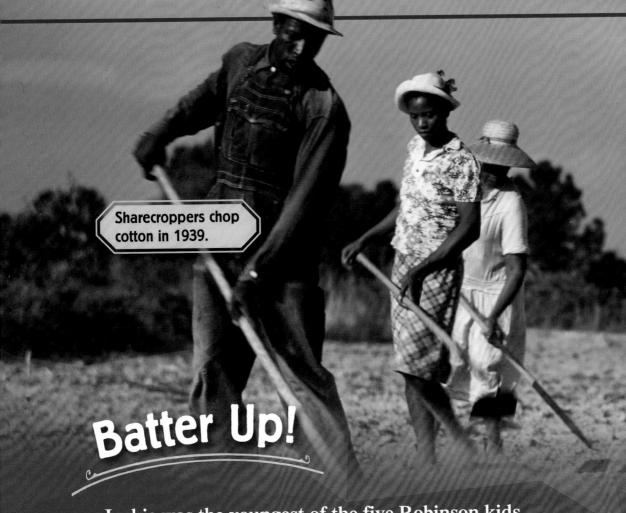

Sharecroppers chop cotton in 1939.

Batter Up!

Jackie was the youngest of the five Robinson kids. Their parents were Jerry and Mallie. The two had a hard time making ends meet. They were poor sharecroppers in Georgia.

Sharecroppers rent land from a farmer. They grow crops on the land. Then, they give some of the crops to the farmer. There is not much left over for them. Nobody gets rich as a sharecropper!

young Jackie Robinson

When Jackie was a baby, his father left the family. Jerry was the main **earner**. Mallie and the kids grew poorer. They could not make it on their own. They moved to California. Mallie's brother had a small house there. The family moved in with him.

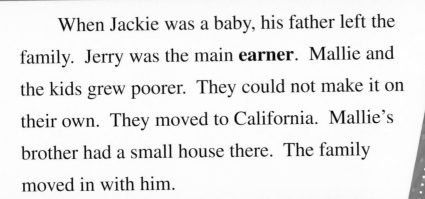

Home of the Rose Parade

Jackie moved to Pasadena, California. This is the home of the Tournament of Roses Parade. It is held on New Year's Day.

Jackie's childhood home

Mack

Edgar

Frank

Jackie

Willa Mae

Mallie (mother)

Jackie's family

They were the only black family on the block. Many people around them did not like black people. They were **prejudiced** (PREJ-uh-dist). They tried to make the family leave. Times were hard. But Mallie was tough. She worked hard and helped the family stand strong. The hard times made the family grow closer.

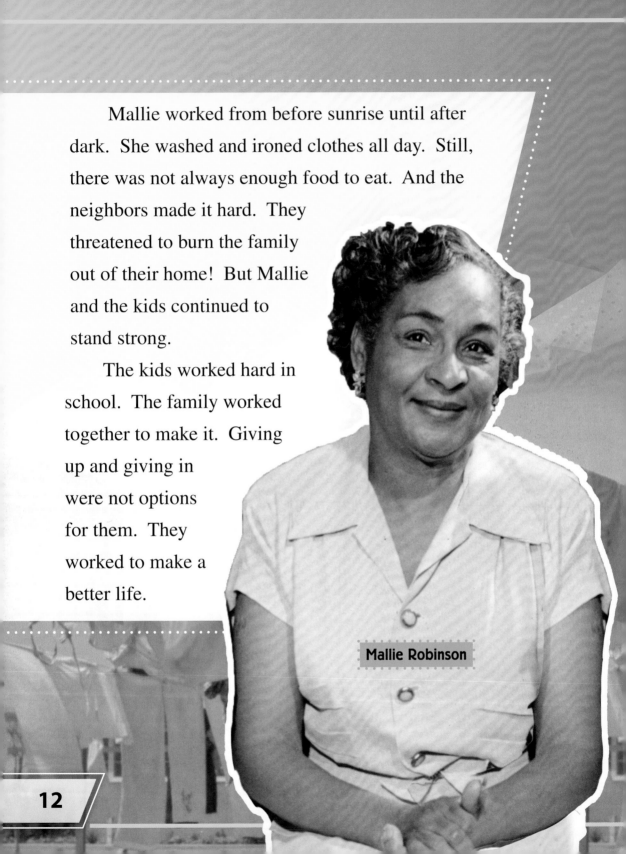

Mallie worked from before sunrise until after dark. She washed and ironed clothes all day. Still, there was not always enough food to eat. And the neighbors made it hard. They threatened to burn the family out of their home! But Mallie and the kids continued to stand strong.

The kids worked hard in school. The family worked together to make it. Giving up and giving in were not options for them. They worked to make a better life.

Mallie Robinson

JACKIE ROBINSON
RESIDED ON THIS SITE WITH HIS
FAMILY FROM 1922 TO 1946

Pepper Street

Jackie and his family lived on Pepper Street in Pasadena, California. There is now a plaque (PLAK) that celebrates the time he lived there.

Jackie was a good kid, but he started to have some trouble. He found friends that called themselves the Pepper Street Gang. They were bad news for Jackie.

Mallie and the kids belonged to Scott Methodist (METH-uhd-ihst) Church. The pastor there was Reverend Karl Downs. Rev. Downs wanted to help. Jackie was missing **guidance** and love from his father. Rev. Downs tried to help fill that need for Jackie. He helped Jackie stay on track.

Reverend Karl Downs

Mentor

Rev. Downs was a mentor to Jackie. A mentor teaches, guides, listens to, and supports someone. A mentor helps a person do and be his or her best.

Running the Bases

Jackie loved sports all his life. He earned a **letter** in four sports in high school! He played the same four sports in junior college. Then he went to UCLA. That is a college in California. There, he earned letters in all four sports again!

While in college, Jackie stood up against **racism** (RAY-sihz-uhm) many times. Once, he was arrested for it. He spoke up for a friend who was wrongfully stopped by the police. Jackie knew that all people should have the same rights. He was willing to stand strong to make the world a better place for everyone.

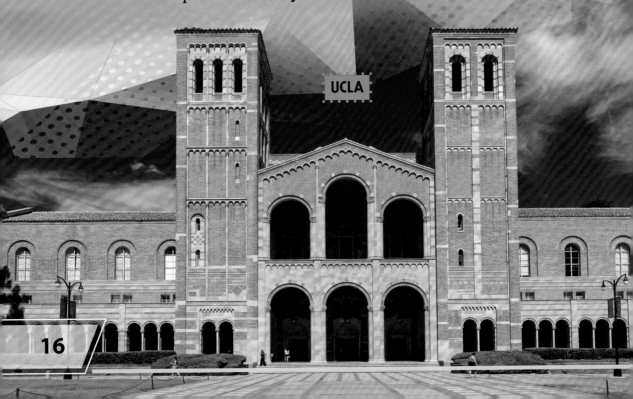

UCLA

Four-Sport Superstar!

Jackie played well in four different sports: baseball, basketball, football, and track. He was an all-around star athlete.

This segregated bus station had a separate waiting room for African Americans in 1940.

Jackie was not able to finish his classes at UCLA. He moved to Hawaii instead to play football for an **integrated** team. But that did not last long. World War II got in the way.

Jackie joined the U.S. Army. But he never fought overseas. Instead, he was arrested while he was in boot camp in Texas. He refused to give up his seat on a bus to a white person. At the time, Texas was **segregated**. Jackie had to give up his seat. He knew it was wrong. He would not do it.

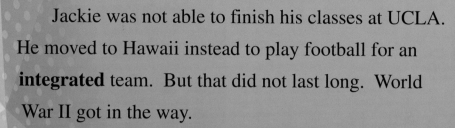

Court-Marshal

A court-marshal is a military court. The court-marshal tried Jackie because he would not give up his seat on the bus. After the trial, Jackie was sent to a new unit.

The Home Stretch

After the war, Jackie went back to sports. He joined the Negro Baseball League. Back then, black and white players did not play together.

In 1946, Jackie married Rachel Isum. They had met in school. They were happy.

Then, Jackie got a call from the Brooklyn Dodgers. The Dodgers were a great team! But all the players were white. Jackie was a great player. The team wanted him. But it would be hard. Many people did not want integration.

Jackie and Rachel thought about it. They knew it was the right thing to do. Jackie joined the Dodgers.

Rachel and Jackie had three children: Jackie Jr., Sharon, and David.

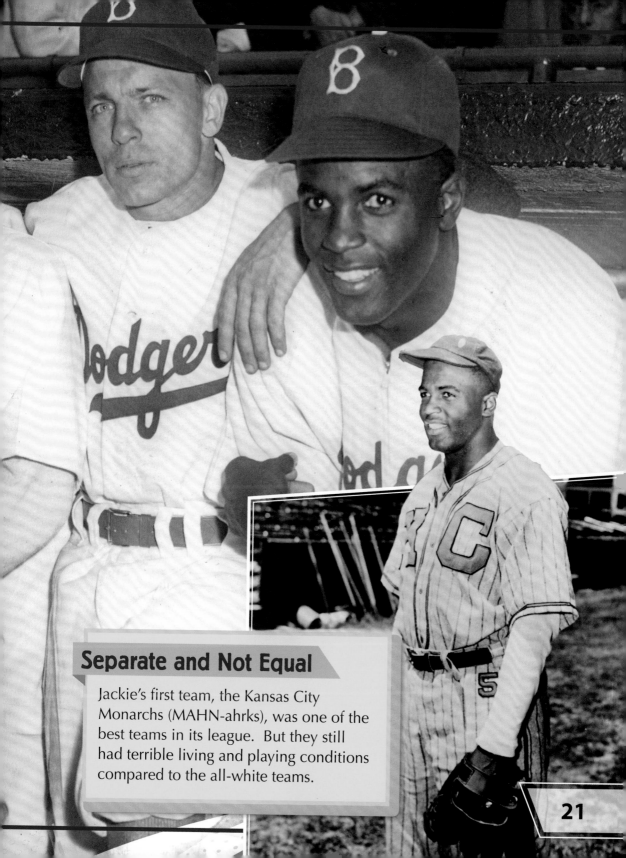

Separate and Not Equal

Jackie's first team, the Kansas City Monarchs (MAHN-ahrks), was one of the best teams in its league. But they still had terrible living and playing conditions compared to the all-white teams.

Playing in the all-white league was more than hard. It was nearly impossible. Jackie was called names. People threw things at him. They threatened his life. But he could not fight back. To change things, he had to remain calm and play well, no matter what.

It was hard. But Jackie had been fighting for **equality** (ih-KWAHL-uh-tee) all his life. He made a stand. The hard times pushed him harder. He became a better player than ever before! Jackie was named Rookie of the Year. He also led the league in stolen bases and was one of baseball's best hitters.

Dodger president Branch Rickey said he was looking for a player with "guts enough *not* to fight back."

Dodger boss Rickey realized a lifelong ambition when he broke baseball's color line by signing Jackie Robinson (below). Behind Rickey is a picture of Abe

A Branch Grows in Brooklyn

Branch Rickey flourishes in Flatbush, champions the Negro in baseball, and is the father of major league's profitable farm system

By TIM COHANE

Wesley Branch Rickey, 64-year-old president of the Brooklyn Dodgers, enjoys an indifferent press. Some sportswriters roar regularly for his head to be brought in on home plate, preferably with a baseball in his mouth as a gag in the literal sense. Others are less bloodthirsty.

"Branch has so got into the habit of quoting scripture," these latter point out, "that even when his mo-

tives are purely altruistic, his critics are still dubi

Most Tongmen and Pollyannas alike, however, Rickey in print or in private when he brought the into modern organized baseball for the first time re by signing Jackie Robinson, a shortstop, to a co with the Dodgers' farm team at Montreal.

Nobody could reasonably suspect materialisti tives. Negro stars are not imperative to the pennant labors toward, nor could they improve attendance bets Field where a third-place team played to over lion paying fans last season.

In fact, signing Robinson may cost Rickey mon Branch is about as allergic to money as he is to F Already, talent bird dogs have routed young pro away from Brooklyn, because (Continued on

Jackie Robinson

70 LOOK MARCH 19

The Jackie Robinson Award is presented to the American League Rookie of the Year.

JACKIE ROBINSON AWARD

2006
ROOKIE OF THE YEAR
AMERICAN LEAGUE

PRESENTED TO

Jackie's success grew. He was a batting champ. One year, he was named Most Valuable Player. The wall between players came down. But it had cost Jackie. He had to hold back his own anger. That was hard on him.

But Jackie was glad about his **legacy**. More players of color joined baseball and other sports, too. Jackie opened the doors. He was proud of that.

Jackie left the sport after 10 years. He was voted into the Baseball Hall of Fame.

But Jackie did not live long. He suffered from a terrible illness. At age 53, Jackie died.

Dr. Martin Luther King Jr. is said to have reached out to Jackie for advice.

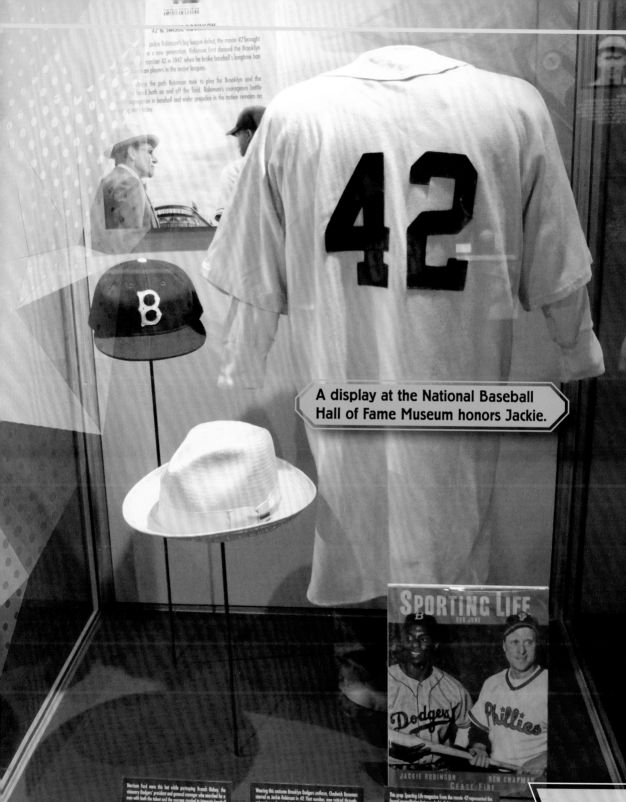

A display at the National Baseball Hall of Fame Museum honors Jackie.

Sliding Home!

Jackie left a legacy for all time. He opened doors for all players to come.

The great Dodger Tommy Davis, who signed with the team because of Jackie, was asked what Jackie meant to him. Tommy said, "He was the right person at the right time to do what he had to do for all the rest of us. He was patient enough to withstand it." Tommy added, "All I can say is thank you."*

Thank you, Jackie! You are a hero for us all. The world can never forget Number 42.

*quoted from author's interview with Davis on July 26, 2015

Jackie Robinson Foundation

In 1973, Jackie's wife, Rachel, started the Jackie Robinson Foundation. It supports students with challenges and gives scholarships. The foundation helps about 250 students each year.

Tommy Davis

The Jackie Robinson Foundation
ROBIE Award for Achievement in Industry
Thomas Tull
March 1, 2013

Ask It!

Tommy Davis is a baseball champ. As a Dodger, he was the league RBI (runs batted in) champ once. He was the league batting champ twice. He was an All-Star three times. And he helped his team win the 1963 World Series!

Read what Tommy says about Jackie. Then, interview one of your heroes. Share your interview with your friends.

When I saw him [Jackie], I wanted to become a baseball player.

Tommy Davis

Interviewer: What impact did Jackie Robinson have on your career in baseball?

Tommy: "He came up in the Brooklyn Dodgers in 1947, and he created a big storm of talent. Everyone drew to him. I was about eight years old when he came up. When I saw him, I wanted to become a baseball player."

Interviewer: Is it true that Jackie influenced you to become a Dodger?

Tommy: "It is true. I signed out of high school. Five or six teams approached me. One team was the Yankees. They showed me a lot of attention…. Al Campanis of the Dodgers found out I was going to sign with the Yankees on a Tuesday night. They had Jackie Robinson call me on the Sunday before the Tuesday. I recognized his voice immediately. He had that high voice. He told me I should sign with the Dodgers. I signed with them on Tuesday."

Interviewer: What do you think Jackie would most like to be remembered for?

Tommy: "Standing up for equal rights for everyone so they could all have an equal chance."

Glossary

earner—someone who works for money

equality—being treated in the same way and having the same rights

guidance—help or advice that tells you what to do

hero—a person who is brave and who people look up to

integrated—allowing all types of people to be included

legacy—something that happened or that comes from someone in the past

letter—a badge, usually with a letter of the alphabet, given to reward an athlete on a sports team and sewn onto a special jacket or sweater

prejudiced—having unfair feelings and dislike against something or someone

racism—the belief that some races of people are better than others

segregated—to have separated groups of people because of their race or religion

Index

Your Turn!

Advice from Others

It is said that Martin Luther King Jr. asked Jackie for advice. What advice do you think Jackie gave to him? Write a letter with the advice that Jackie may have sent to Martin.